Spring

Claire Llewellyn

SIMON & SCHUSTER
YOUNG BOOKS

Notes for parents and teachers

This book has a theme that threads its way through the subject of the book. It does not aim to deal with the topic comprehensively; rather it aims to provoke thought and discussion. Each page heading makes a simple statement about the illustration which is then amplified and questioned by the text. Material in this book is particularly relevant to the following sections of the National Curriculum for England and Wales:

English: AT1 levels 1–2, AT2 levels 1–3
Geography: AT5 levels 1–3
Science: AT2 levels 1–3, AT9 levels 1–2, AT16 levels 1–3

In Scotland the proposals of the Scottish Education Department apply.

TAKE ONE has been researched and compiled by Simon & Schuster Young Books. We are very grateful for the support and guidance provided by our advisory panel of professional educationalists in the course of the production.

Advisory panel:
Colin Pidgeon, Headteacher
Wheatfields Junior School, St Albans
Deirdre Walker, Deputy headteacher
Wheatfields Junior School, St Albans
Judith Clarke, Headteacher
Grove Infants School, Harpenden

Commissioning editor: Daphne Butler
Design: M&M Design Partnership
Photographs: ZEFA cover and pages 6, 11, 12 (top and bottom right), 14, 15, 19, 23 and 27; Ecoscene pages 7, 8, 12 (top and bottom left), 16, 22, 24 and 29; Heather Angel pages 10, 18 and 20.

First published in Great Britain in 1992 by Simon & Schuster Young Books

Simon & Schuster Young Books
Campus 400, Maylands Avenue
Hemel Hempstead, Herts HP2 7EZ

© 1992 Simon & Schuster Young Books

A catalogue record for this book is available from the British Library
ISBN 0 7500 1033 9

Printed and bound in Great Britain by BPCC Hazell Books, Paulton and Aylesbury

Contents

Spring is coming

How can you tell that spring is coming?

The weather may still be cold outside but, if you look closely, you will notice certain changes.

What are they?

7

8

The days are getting longer

Each spring morning the sun rises
earlier than it did the day before.
Each evening it sets a little later.

The sun is higher in the sky.
Day by day, the weather gets brighter
and a little warmer.   Why is this?

Many animals breed now

Spring is a good time to have babies.

Why?   What do babies need to survive?

11

12

Birds are busy

Do you sometimes hear the birds
singing very early on spring mornings?
Spring is a busy time for them.   They
may raise not just one family, but two.

You don't need to see a bird on its
nest to know it's breeding.   What
other signs are there?

Young animals grow and learn

Young mammals feed on their mother's milk.   They grow quickly.

They play with their brothers and sisters.   This makes them stronger, and is one of the ways they learn about hunting and fighting.

Ponds come to life

Many creatures rest at the bottom of a pond during winter.   As the spring sun warms the water, they begin to stir.

Frogs breed in the spring.   They lay eggs, called spawn, in the water. What hatches from the spawn?

Everything begins to grow

Spring sun and rain make the ground warm and moist.   This is just what seeds, grasses, plants and trees need in order to grow.

Spring is a busy time for farmers and gardeners.   What jobs are there to do?

19

20

Buds burst on the trees

Trees have buds on their branches all through the winter.

Some buds are like tightly-packed parcels.   Inside are the leaves and the flowers, ready to grow.

Why don't buds grow in winter?   What is it that makes them burst?

A time of flowers

Think of all the different spring flowers there are.   Even in deserts, spring rains make the flowers bloom.

Trees and hedgerows blossom in town and country.   Do you know why some trees have blossom and others don't?

23

24

Insects are active

Bees, butterflies and other insects rest during the winter.   Warm spring days make them active again.

They find food in the colourful, sweet-smelling flowers in meadows, woods and gardens.

Visiting insects can help plants. Do you know how?

Out and about

After the cold, dark days of winter
it's wonderful to play or work outside
in the fresh air.

How do you and your friends enjoy
the spring?

Summer is coming

The season is changing.   All the
leaves have opened on the trees, and
the blossom has faded.   The days are
becoming longer and hotter.

Why do the seasons change?   Why does
summer always follow spring?

Index